Better Homes and Gardens®

50 Boo-tiful Halloween Full-Size Patterns

AND 100 TRICKS FOR USING THEM

Better Homes and Gardens® Books
Des Moines, Iowa

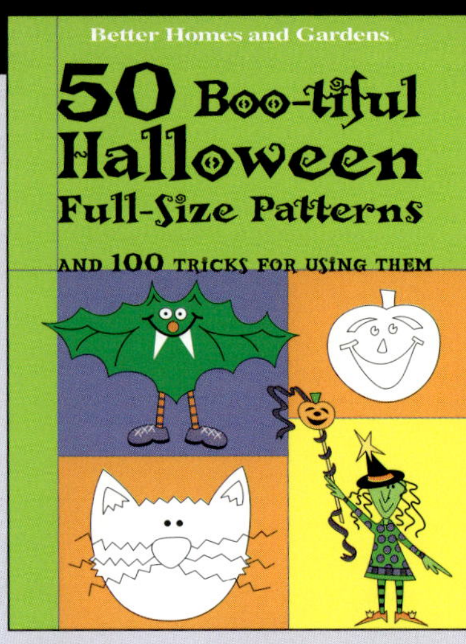

An imprint of Meredith® Books

50 Boo-tiful Halloween Full-Size Patterns and 100 Tricks for Using Them

Editor: Carol Field Dahlstrom
Contributing Editor: Susan Banker
Graphic Designer: Angela Hoogensen
Copy Chief: Terri Fredrickson
Copy and Production Editor: Victoria Forlini
Editorial Operations Manager: Karen Schirm
Managers, Book Production: Pam Kvitne,
    Marjorie J. Schenkelberg
Contributing Copy Editor: Maria Duryée
Contributing Proofreader: Gretchen Kauffman
Technical Illustrator: Chris Neubauer Graphics, Inc.
Electronic Production Coordinator: Paula Forest
Editorial and Design Assistants: Kaye Chabot,
    Mary Lee Gavin, Karen McFadden

Meredith® Books
Publisher and Editor in Chief: James D. Blume
Design Director: Matt Strelecki
Managing Editor: Gregory H. Kayko
Executive Editor, Food and Crafts:
    Jennifer Dorland Darling

Director, Operations: George A. Susral
Director, Production: Douglas M. Johnston

Vice President and General Manager:
    Douglas J. Guendel

Meredith Publishing Group
President, Publishing Group: Stephen M. Lacy
Vice President-Publishing Director: Bob Mate

Meredith Corporation
Chairman and Chief Executive Officer:
    William T. Kerr

Chairman of the Executive Committee:
    E. T. Meredith III

Pattern Illustrations: Susan Banker, Carol
    Dahlstrom, Alice Wetzel

100 Uses for Halloween Patterns

These patterns can be used at the size given or they can be enlarged or reduced on a photocopier. Depending on your project, you can use one or a combination of several of the designs.

To trace the patterns, we recommend one of two techniques. Place tracing paper over the pattern and trace the lines. Or place the book pattern page on a light source, such as a light box or taped to a sunny window, and trace the pattern onto printer paper.

To transfer the designs, you can cut out the traced pattern and draw around it. Or place transfer paper between the pattern and the object to which you wish to transfer the design.

Decorating Pumpkins

1. Use simple patterns for carving inspiration.
2. Transfer pattern to pumpkin and paint with enamel paint. Paint the lines black and let dry. Paint in areas with desired colors.
3. Outline simple shapes in black permanent marker. Paint white glue or decoupage medium between the lines and sprinkle with glitter. If you wish to use more than one color of glitter, let one area dry before using another color.
4. Transfer a pattern outline to a pumpkin. Press small pins into the pumpkin following the outline.
5. Paint a pattern on a pumpkin using metallic fingernail polish.
6. Cut pattern pieces from crafting foam; pin in place.
7. Draw pumpkin faces on miniature pumpkins or gourds and color in with permanent marker.

Painting Glass and Ceramic
Use paints designed specifically for glass.

8. For tumblers, place a traced pattern inside a clear glass. On the outside, paint the lines black and fill in with desired colors.
9. For plates, tape the design right side down on a clear glass plate top. Paint the bottom of the plate, starting with fine black outlines. Fill in with color.
10. Mix-and-match water and wine goblets work well for Halloween potions. Paint each one with a different design so guests know which glass is theirs.
11. Paint tiny designs on a cup or mug for those who prefer hot concoctions, such as coffin coffee or hair-raising hot chocolate.
12. For a Halloween goody jar, tape a pattern inside a

clear glass cookie jar.
Paint the desired motif
on the outside.

13. Transfer a design to a
ceramic tile. Paint design
and let dry. Display the
tile on a plate stand.

14. Remove the glass from
a serving tray. Tape the
desired motif to one side
of the glass. Paint the
lines black and let dry.
Paint in the areas. Let
dry. Reassemble the tray,
paint side on the bottom.

15. Paint a small design on
a votive candleholder.

Haunted House Decorations

16. Paint Halloween designs
in windows with stained
glass removable paints.

17. Use simple patterns to
cut shapes from felt. Use
blanket stitch to secure
the pieces in place on a
decorative pillow top.

18. Using Halloween fabrics,
cut pattern pieces
from the desired
design. Following
the manufacturer's
instructions, use
transweb paper to
adhere the pieces to a
tablecloth or tablerunner.
Finish the edges with
machine embroidery.

19. For lawn decorations,
enlarge character
patterns, such as a witch
or Frankenstein, to be
approximately 3–5 feet
tall. Transfer the pattern
to wood and cut out.
Paint in the details
using enamel.

20. Paint a design on a
plain welcome mat for a
clever door entrance.

21. Trace a simple pattern
onto adhesive vinyl. Cut
out the shapes (making a
stencil) on a protected
work surface using a
crafts knife. Peel off

backing and place on a
glass cylinder vase or
canister. Brush etching
cream over the open
areas. Etch the design
following the
manufacturer's directions.

22. Cut patterns from black
paper and tape to the
outside of flat
lampshades. Replace the
bulbs with low-watt bulbs
for Halloween silhouettes.

23. Paint a design on a
plastic cauldron and use
to serve punch.

24. Make a large stencil from
a ghost or skeleton
pattern. Place the stencil
on a window and spray
with artificial canned
snow for windows.

25. Cut designs from black
paper and tape to
windows. Place a light
source behind the cutouts
so the silhouettes are
visible from the exterior.

26. Use permanent markers
to add designs to empty
milk jug luminarias.

27. Transfer mini patterns to
place cards and color in
with markers.

28. Make a wood welcome
sign to post by your door.

29. Use small patterns to
cut designs into crepe
paper streamers.

30. Cut tissue paper designs
and tape to mirrors
and windows for a
haunting effect.

31. Use permanent marking
pens to draw simple
designs on balloons.

32. Cut Halloween shapes
from construction
paper and glue on a
party hat.

33. Make place mats from
paper or crafting foam.

34. Use enlarged patterns to
make paper decorations.

35. Paint or draw designs on
foam coasters.

36. Cut stencil-shape designs
from lunch sacks and use
as luminarias.

Furniture

37. For a fun side table,
transfer a pattern to
heavy white paper. Paint
the design. Make several
colored photocopies of the
painted design. Decoupage
a design in the center of
the table.

38. Pick up flea market
chairs and paint with
Halloween designs.
Alternate the eerie chairs
with your regular ones
for the haunting season.

39. Paint an ornate mirror
frame black and sprinkle
with silver glitter. Let dry.
Paint a ghost or skeleton
on the mirror using white
glass paint.

40. Make a jack-o'-lantern
stand by painting motifs
on a step stool.

Trick-or-Treat Wear

41. Paint or appliqué a design
on a tote bag.

42. Paint a silk scarf with
Halloween motifs.

43. Create a pair of
Halloween tennis shoes
by outlining designs on
white shoes.

44. Use the patterns as
inspiration for making
trick-or-treating costumes.

45. Paint designs on a denim
jumper or skirt.

46. Make clay pins using
the Halloween patterns
as guides.

47. Enlarge face patterns
to make masks from
crafting foam.

48. Use the designs for
face painting inspiration.

49. Make wire earrings using
designs as inspirations.

continued on page 4

50. Use fabric paint to create a design on a sweatshirt.

Goody Holders

51. Paint a design on the lid and around the side of a papier-mâché box.
52. Paint a design on a plain sand pail.
53. Decoupage a design on a tin can.
54. Paint designs on a small vase and fill with candy sticks or suckers.
55. Glue cut-paper designs on vellum envelopes.
56. Cut shapes from felt and glue onto a lunch bag.
57. Make a treat pouch from crafting foam.
58. Embroider a design on a doll-size pillowcase.
59. Paint designs parading around a terra-cotta or glass flowerpot.
60. Use enamel paints to add a design to an unused gallon paint can.
61. Cut a stencil-style design from a paper bag and back with colored cellophane.
62. Use fabric glue to adhere fabric cutouts to a marble bag (available at game stores).
63. Paint a design on a small tote or purse.
64. Cut designs from paper and glue to a gift bag.
65. Cut a paper strip to fit inside a jar. Draw designs on the paper. With the designs on the outside, roll the paper into a tube. Insert the paper into the jar and let it unroll to fill the jar.

Paper Projects

66. Using card stock, make greeting cards and invites.
67. Create paper mats to frame Halloween photos.
68. Make small designs and glue magnets to the back for the refrigerator.
69. Make a bookmark to accompany a gift of a Halloween book.
70. Use designs to enhance Halloween pages in a scrapbook or album.

Stitchery Projects

71. Transfer a design to a piece of gridded paper and chart your own cross-stitch or needlework design.
72. Embroider a small design on a necktie.
73. Embellish the corners of a tablecloth with embroidery.
74. Stitch a witch on the pocket of a denim shirt.

For the Kids

75. Transfer designs to bright paper and let kids add the color details with crayons or washable markers.
76. Outline a design on a T-shirt. Let a child use fabric markers to color the design as desired.
77. Trace a design on the back of a paper plate and make a mask.
78. Let children try to copy the patterns outdoors using sidewalk chalk.

Gift Ideas

79. Paint a vase and fill with seasonal flowers.
80. Paint a row of characters on the lid of a candy box.
81. Make stenciled wrapping paper for a Halloween gift.
82. Draw a matching gift card.
83. Paint a design on a paper cup and fill it with money.
84. Paint small wood cutouts and hot-glue to a grapevine wreath.
85. To make a jewelry pin, choose a simple design and cut the outside shape from mat board. Paint the details. Glue a bar pin on the back.
86. Appliqué fabric motifs on a warm wool blanket.
87. Add fabric appliqués to the front of a sweatshirt.
88. Use the patterns to inspire a Halloween piñata.
89. Stencil on a large rock for a paperweight, doorstop, or garden embellishment.
90. Choose a design as inspiration to make a plantpoke from clay.
91. Draw pumpkin faces on oranges and place in an assorted fruit basket.
92. Use tube-style paints to draw designs on a cellophane bag and fill with treats.
93. Decorate toys, such as paddleball paddles, throwing disks, or plastic bowling pins.
94. Paint designs on a miniature wagon and fill with goodies.
95. Cut leaf shapes from window screen and paint the edges with tube-style paint.
96. Paint a design in black on an orange gazing ball.
97. Make a storybook and use the designs for the illustrations.
98. Create a character from wood to perch on a mantel or shelf.
99. To add to a child's dress-up wardrobe, make a simple cape and machine appliqué with silhouette-type designs.
100. Paint a design on heavy paper; mat and frame it.

Cats & Bats

Hissing, swooping, loop-d'-looping—
these crazy characters will have you
prowling for projects to use their
clever designs!

BOO!

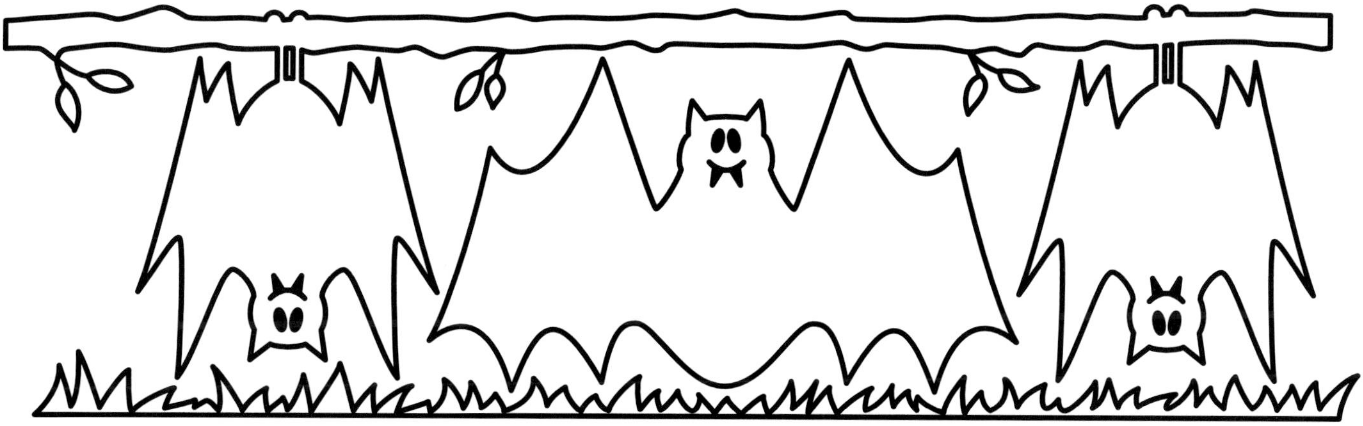

Pumpkins, All Sorts

Carved, drawn, or out on the lawn—
your pumpkins will be the envy of
the neighborhood!

3

Witches, Ghosts, & Skeletons

Cackles, boos, and friendly yoo-hoos—
this gathering of Halloween pranksters
will make you giggle or scare the
dickens out of you!

Favorite Halloween Motifs

Owls in trees, candy corn, if you please—
a cauldron full of "eerie-sistible" designs
awaits in this pattern-packed chapter.

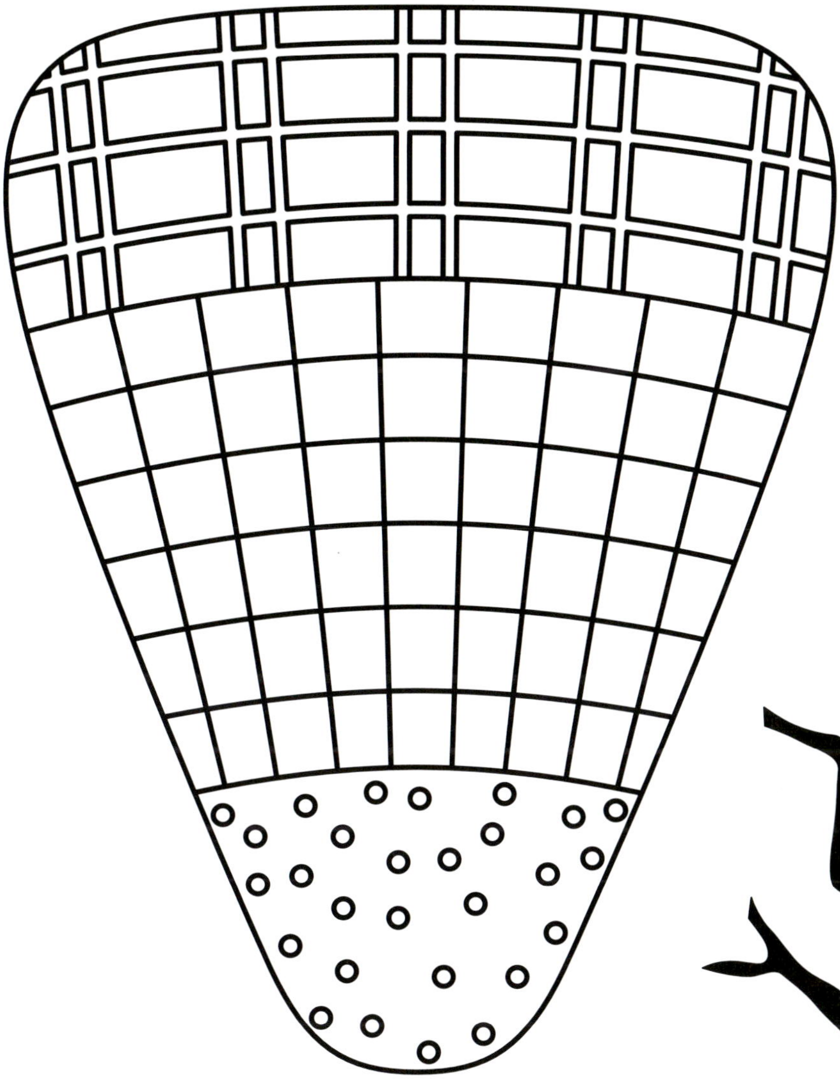

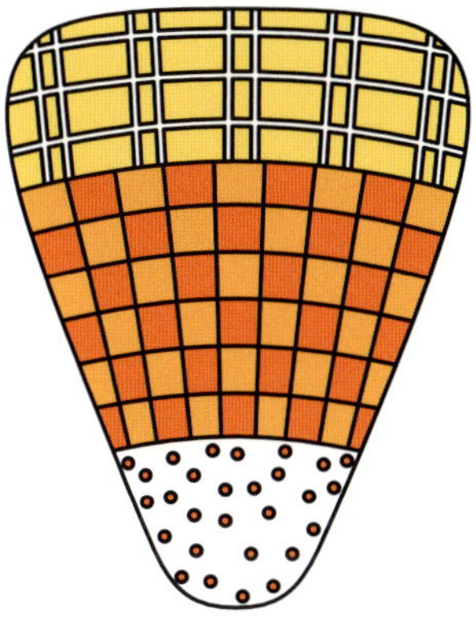